IN THIS EDITION

7 Dr. Karen Semien-McBride: Empowering Women to Lead with Confidence and Clarity

By Rachel Dares

13 Doctor. Leader. Visionary. Dr. Katarzyna Tesmer's Path To Purpose

18 Talk Billing With C&T Podcast

19 Entrepreneurship, Empowerment, and the POWER of OneWomen's Yes

By Amy Chinian

26 Fierce & Fearless Entrepreneur: Dr. Tywanna Smith

30 Thriving in the Grey: The Realisty of Being A Disabled Businesswoman with Chronic Illness

By Andrea Cennington, MSW, LCSW, LCSW-C, LICSW, QS

31 Write The Book Build A Legacy

By Gina Stockdall

32 The Balanced Hustle: Navigating Life as a Woman Entrepreneur

By Chinyere Iroanya

34 Beyond the Paper: How One Coach Helps Parents Use the IEP as a Roadmap to Adulthood

By: Susan Tatem, Founder of Bright Path Coaching

37 Finding Your Power and Beauty After Trauma

By Sonia Rodrigues, Psychotherapist and Founder of Transition to Wellness

39 Beyond Burnout: Self-Care for the Woman Who Does It All

By Lakeisha Lee

29 Back to School, Back to Balance: Helping Kids Thrive Emotionally and Academically

By Shona Royce M.Ed,LPCC, NCC

IN THIS EDITION

44 **Accelerating Success: How Syeda is Redefining Online Sales for Coaches**
By Syeda Iqra

45 **The Woman in the Mirror: From Trauma to Triumph**
By Ciara Lewis

49 **Sparkle, Sip & Win**
By RNR D2 Summit

50 **Rachel Dares PR**

51 **Fierce, Fearless & Unfiltered Podcast**
By Ciara Lewis

52 **Nouvo Studios Miami Free Photoshoot QR Code**

54 **The Power Within Anthology Ad**
By Saskia Christian

55 **Resilience Counseling Services**

56 **Charise Tolls Insurance Broker**

57 **Dear Daughter: Your Story Was Never Meant To Stay Silent**
By Gina Stockdall

58 **The Anchor Holds**
By Ciara Lewis

59 **Become A Published Author**
By Ciara Lewis

60 **School Is In Session**
By Maria Crabtree

Photo Credit: Brandis Images by Brandi | Located in Bowling Green, KY | www.facebook.com/share/1EPHlcqF4u/?mibextid=wwXlfr

FIERCE & FEARLESS MAGAZINE
AUGUST 2025

Letter From The Founder

Dear Readers,

Welcome to the August 2025 edition of Fierce & Fearless Magazine! As we embrace the vibrant summer days, we are excited to bring you a collection of powerful stories, insightful perspectives, and practical advice designed to enhance your path to success and inspire your professional endeavors.

In this issue, we will explore the Top 10 challenges faced by entrepreneurs. We will also feature an inspiring interview with Ciara Lewis, founder and CEO of a Medical Billing and Credentialing Business, who has also ventured into authorship. She will share her journey and the strategic decisions that propelled her into entrepreneurship.

Beyond Ciara's impactful story, this issue will include additional narratives from other successful female entrepreneurs. You will gain insight into their daily routines, the challenges they have overcome, and the valuable tips and advice they have to share. We are eager to present these empowering stories to support other women entrepreneurs as they strive for greater achievements.

Fierce & Fearless is dedicated to providing a platform for women to showcase their courageous career moves, document their fearless journeys, impart industry-specific advice, and offer insights from bold leaders. Our mission is to encourage those who may be hesitant to take bold risks and to take that next significant step. We aim to foster a supportive community, assuring you that you are not alone on this journey.

Thank you for supporting our mission. We hope you find this issue both beneficial and uplifting.

Ciara Lewis
Founder & Editor-In-Chief
Fierce & Fearless Magazine

DR. KAREN SEMIEN-MCBRIDE: EMPOWERING WOMEN TO LEAD WITH CONFIDENCE AND CLARITY

BY: RACHEL DARES

Dr. Karen Semien-McBride uniquely blends the disciplines of psychology and business, harnessing over 25 years of expertise to revolutionize the way leaders—particularly women—navigate growth and leadership. As the founder and CEO of MK Circle Enterprises and The CEO Institute, Dr. McBride has dedicated her career to empowering individuals and organizations to reach their full potential through transformative leadership development, executive coaching, and strategic consulting.

Her journey into entrepreneurship was sparked by a simple yet profound moment: a business card. "My dad worked in a factory, but his real passion was being a DJ. He handed me his business card once, and I remember thinking, 'I want a business card too.' That moment lit a fire in me that led me to start my first business in sixth grade, selling candy," Dr. McBride shares. This early entrepreneurial spirit continued through her teenage years, when she started and sold a flower business for $11,000 at just 17. Her parents—especially her father's passion and her mother's creativity—shaped Dr. McBride's path to entrepreneurship—a path that, despite corporate success, always felt like her true calling.

Dr. McBride's personal experience navigating corporate spaces, particularly as a Black woman, has fueled her passion for empowering others. She recalls, "Early in my career, a company president walked past me and later remarked, 'She seems smart. Hard to believe she's Black.'" Instead of allowing anger to consume her, Dr. McBride chose a strategy and used the moment to change the narrative. "Every encounter is a chance to shift perceptions," she says, stressing the importance of action over reaction.

That strategic mindset is the cornerstone of her work at MK Circle Enterprises, where Dr. McBride helps individuals—particularly women leaders—build sustainable growth through self-awareness, emotional regulation, and strategic positioning. She emphasizes the importance of knowing yourself, your strengths, and your blind spots. "Self-awareness and emotional regulation are key," Dr. McBride asserts. "Leaders need to understand themselves. Are you relational or task-oriented? Are you a conceptual thinker or detail-driven? Being clear on these things can shape your leadership style and decision-making."

Her approach to leadership is holistic, acknowledging that personal and professional lives are intricately intertwined. "You're human. You bring everything with you—your personal life, your upbringing, your emotions. You can't separate them. That's why I studied psychology," she reflects. It's this blend of human behavior understanding and business acumen that allows Dr. McBride to guide her clients through the complexities of leadership, especially when it comes to the unique challenges faced by women entrepreneurs.

One of the key messages Dr. McBride conveys is the importance of stepping into the role of CEO, even from day one. "The moment you start a business, you are the CEO—whether you're baking cookies in your kitchen or running a multi-million-dollar enterprise," she explains. However, she acknowledges that many entrepreneurs resist formalizing their business plans. "A business plan is clarity—it's not just paperwork. It helps you define your direction: Are you building a million-dollar company or just supporting your family? That clarity is crucial," Dr. McBride advises.

DR. KAREN SEMIEN-MCBRIDE: EMPOWERING WOMEN TO LEAD WITH CONFIDENCE AND CLARITY

By Rachel Dares

Also champions the importance of pricing and how many entrepreneurs—particularly women—underprice their services. "You need to factor in your time, labor, and expertise. If you had to pay someone else to do what you're doing, how much would it cost?"

Dr. McBride challenges entrepreneurs to value their time and expertise accordingly, which is why she's made it a part of her mission to help small business owners develop pitch decks that lay the foundation for a full business plan.

For Dr. McBride, the most rewarding aspect of her work is watching women grow into their leadership potential. "My legacy is to help women understand their worth and to stand in their power, no matter what," she says. "I want them to know who they are, to be aware of their power, and to use that power strategically. That's how we change the narrative."

Beyond leadership coaching, Dr. McBride is also an advocate for women supporting one another in business. "Women need to support each other more," she says, calling out the all-too-common reluctance to share opportunities or refer other women for business. "We should be building referral networks, supporting one another's businesses. The more we support each other, the more we all thrive."

In addition to being the CEO of her company, Dr. McBride is set to release her new book, *Lead with Style*, which is based on her operational style theory. This book is designed to help leaders harness their unique operational leadership style to succeed in both business and life.

With plans for additional volumes focused on relationships, women, and more, Lead with Style is just the first step in Dr. McBride's mission to transform the leadership journey—how it is understood and practiced.

As Dr. McBride continues to inspire and equip women entrepreneurs to lead with clarity, confidence, and purpose, she is building a legacy of empowerment that will ripple through generations.

Her work is a testament to the power of self-awareness, strategy, and community support—values that are shaping a new generation of leaders who will thrive unapologetically.

Dr. Karen Semien-McBride's Legacy

Dr. McBride's message to women in business is simple: Know your worth, step into your power, and lead with clarity. As she continues to break down barriers and create space for women leaders, she is paving the way for the next generation of fierce and fearless entrepreneurs.

Website: www.mkcircle.com
LinkedIn: Dr. Karen Semien-McBride

Photo Credit: Brandis Images by Brandi | Located in Bowling Green, KY | www.facebook.com/share/1EPHcqF4u/?mibextid=wwXIff

LEAD WITH STYLE

DR. KAREN SEMIEN-MCBRIDE

Harnessing Your Operational Style

"Strategies for Effective Leadership Growth and Organizational Culture Shifts"

Dr. Karen L. Semien-McBride

is a renowned social psychologist, executive coach, business strategist, and motivational speaker. As the founder and CEO of MKCircle Enterprises and the CEO Institute, she has dedicated over 25 years to empowering individuals and organizations through leadership development and strategic coaching.

Dr. Semien-McBride's entrepreneurial spirit was evident from a young age, launching her first business at 12 and a successful floral enterprise at 17, funded her higher education. She holds a Bachelor's in Business Administration, a Master's in Management and Organizational Leadership, and multiple doctorates, including in Business Administration/Organizational Psychology and Management & Consulting. Post education she with her husband now own multiple very successful business.

Her academic pursuits led to the creation of the Operational Style Theory, a framework that integrates psychological principles with practical leadership strategies. This theory serves as the cornerstone of her coaching programs and the foundation of this book, offering insights into effective communication, decision-making, and team dynamics.

At the helm of MKCircle Enterprises, LLC and MKCircle CEO Institute, Dr. Semien-McBride has transformed the lives of countless professionals, fostering awareness, regulation and motivated leaders equipped to navigate the complexities of modern organizational landscapes. Her commitment to excellence and innovation continues to inspire growth and transformation across various sectors. More about Dr. Karen's research and development visit **www.mkcircle.com**

Photo Credit: Brandis Images by Brandi | Located in Bowling Green, KY | www.facebook.com/share/1EPHicqF4u/?mibextid=wwXlfr

BECOMING *the Most* SUCCESSFUL YOU!

We offer programs that support the interior and exterior of an organization with planning, executive & mid-management coaching, growth and sustainability strategies. Learn more about our programs at www.mkcircle.com

"Life is not a sport you want to participate in without a coach"

— Dr. Karen Semien-McBride

Visit us today
www.mkcircle.com

HOME OF THE NEW LEADERSHIP LANGUAGE METHOD

SUPPORTING YOU IN:

EXECUTIVE, LEADERSHIP COACHING AND TRAINING

- Mid-level Management & Team Engagement
- Change/Pivot Management & Trainings
- PEAP (Private Employee Assistance Programs)
- Corporate and Individual Counsellings
- And So Much More

DR. KATARZYNA TESMER

Doctor. Leader. Visionary: Dr. Katarzyna Tesmer's Fearless Path to Purpose

Journey to Entrepreneurship

- **What was the moment or event that inspired you to start your entrepreneurial journey?**

The moment that inspired me to start my entrepreneurial journey was a culmination of my desire to make a more direct, lasting impact on my patients' lives. After years of working in neonatal care and saving infants in critical conditions, I felt a growing need to expand my reach and help individuals in a different, yet equally meaningful way—through aesthetic medicine. The ability to restore someone's confidence, help them feel their best, and improve their quality of life was what drove me to open Visage Laser & Skin Care. I wanted to create a space where beauty and well-being were intertwined, where patients could not only look better, but feel empowered in their own skin. This drive to combine my medical expertise with a deeper commitment to people's self-esteem was the foundation of my journey into entrepreneurship.

- **Were there any key challenges you faced early on, and how did you overcome them?**

In the early days of Visage Laser & Skin Care, one of the biggest challenges I faced was balancing my full-time neonatal position, board roles in several organizations, running my medspa, and managing my family life. It was a true juggling act. My family, understandably, wanted me to spend more time with them, and, at times, they even encouraged me to close Visage, fearing I was spreading myself too thin. However, my passion for both neonatal care and aesthetic medicine drove me to keep pushing forward. I had to learn how to manage my time effectively, prioritizing my commitments and making sure I stayed present in each role. Despite the challenges, I remained determined to build Visage while continuing my work in neonatology and serving on various boards. It was difficult, but I focused on staying organized and disciplined, making sure that every decision I made was aligned with my long-term vision. Through sheer perseverance, Visage grew, and over time, I built a strong team that allowed me to take a step back in certain areas of the business. That period taught me important lessons in self-reliance, the value of hard work, and the importance of making sacrifices for the things that truly matter.

- **What were some unexpected hurdles you didn't anticipate when you first launched your business?**

One of the biggest unexpected hurdles I faced was employee turnover. When I first launched Visage Laser & Skin Care, I didn't anticipate how difficult it would be to find a team that truly shared my mission and vision for the business. It wasn't just about finding skilled individuals—it was about finding people who were trustworthy, committed, and aligned with the values of integrity and excellence that are at the core of Visage. Building a cohesive team that understood the importance of patient care, the personalized experience we offer, and the dedication to results took time and patience. I learned that a strong, reliable team is essential for success, and it took many years to cultivate a team that not only believes in our mission but also consistently delivers outstanding care.

Empowerment & Resilience

- **What does being a 'fierce and fearless' woman entrepreneur mean to you personally?**

For me, being a 'fierce and fearless' woman entrepreneur means having a never-give-up attitude. It's about persevering through challenges, no matter how tough they get. There have been many obstacles along the way—whether it's managing a growing business, balancing my career in neonatal care, or dealing with personal sacrifices—but I've always maintained the mindset that failure is not an option. It's about pushing through adversity, staying committed to my vision, and continuously striving to improve. Being fierce and fearless means showing up every day, even when things aren't easy, and never losing sight of the bigger picture.

- **How do you manage the balance between confidence and vulnerability in business?**

Balancing confidence and vulnerability in business is key to maintaining trust and fostering growth. Confidence allows me to lead with conviction, make decisions, and drive Visage Laser & Skin Care forward. I trust in my expertise and the vision I've created for the business.

However, vulnerability is just as important. It's about being open with my team about the status of the business—what we need to do to maintain and grow. I actively encourage feedback and am willing to admit when we've hit challenges. By embracing vulnerability, I can connect with my team and clients, creating a culture of collaboration and continuous improvement. It's this balance that allows me to be a strong leader while also being receptive to the needs of the business and the people I work with.

- **Can you share a moment where you felt completely knocked down and how you managed to bounce back?**

One of the most challenging moments early on was when I trusted a business partner who ultimately took advantage of that trust, causing significant emotional and financial strain. It was a deeply painful experience, especially considering the immense effort I had put into building Visage Laser & Skin Care. However, I refused to let that setback define me. I rebuilt my business from the ground up, learned invaluable lessons about trust and discernment, and emerged stronger than before. Overcoming that moment taught me the importance of resilience and the power of perseverance in the face of adversity.

The second challenge came during the pandemic, when I had to close Visage in response to the global crisis. It was an incredibly difficult period, watching the business I'd worked so hard to build face uncertainty. But I saw this as an opportunity to adapt, rethink how we could continue serving our clients, and find new ways to stay connected. That experience reaffirmed my belief in the importance of staying agile and determined, even in the face of overwhelming adversity.

Both of these moments were tough, but they strengthened my resolve and taught me that setbacks are inevitable. What truly matters is how you choose to rise from them—more focused, more driven, and more discerning in the decisions you make moving forward.

- **How do you maintain motivation during times of self-doubt or when facing criticism?**

Staying true to my vision, keeping a clear sense of purpose, and remembering the bigger picture helps me push forward, even in tough times.

Leadership & Growth

- **What leadership qualities do you believe are essential for women in entrepreneurship?**

For women in entrepreneurship, I believe confidence, knowledge, and integrity are essential.

- **How do you foster a culture of empowerment within your team or business?**

I foster a culture of empowerment by leading through example and maintaining integrity in everything I do. I believe in always doing the right thing, even when it's challenging, and holding myself to the highest standards. By setting that example, I encourage my team to do the same. I also create an environment where everyone has the opportunity to grow and thrive. I believe in recognizing the unique expertise each person brings to the table and empowering them to use it to contribute to the success of the business as a whole.

- **As your business has grown, what have you learned about the art of delegation?**

I've learned that delegation is a must—no one can do it all alone. As Visage Laser & Skin Care has grown, I've recognized the importance of giving my staff the independence to thrive in their roles. I encourage them to take ownership of their work and support their growth. When they achieve their goals, they find satisfaction both personally and professionally, which ultimately contributes to the success of the entire business.

- **How do you prioritize your personal growth alongside the growth of your business?**

It's all about balance. I work hard to ensure success in everything I do, but I also make time for the things that matter most—spending time with family and friends and taking vacations. Work hard, play harder is my approach. Personal growth is just as important as business growth, and by making time for what recharges me, I stay focused, motivated, and inspired to achieve both my professional goals and personal well-being.

Challenges Specific to Women Entrepreneurs

- **What do you think are some of the biggest challenges women face when starting a business, and how do you navigate them?**

One of the biggest challenges women face when starting a business is determining if they have the resilience or staying power to navigate the complexities of building a business financially, emotionally, mentally, and spiritually.

There are so many factors to consider, such as resources, managing time, and covering the financial costs of starting and running a business, which can all feel overwhelming. To navigate these challenges, I encourage women to first build a strong foundation by being clear on their vision and mission. Building a strong foundation from the outset is key. Surrounding themselves with a supportive team, mentors, and advisors helps to tackle obstacles with confidence. No business is built alone—having the right support system in place can make all the difference in managing the challenges of entrepreneurship.

- **Have you faced any gender-related biases in your career, and how did you respond to them?**

I wish gender-related biases were not something I had to face, but unfortunately, I've experienced them, especially here in the U.S. Despite my expertise and experience, there have been times when I've been underestimated or dismissed simply because I'm a woman.

- **In your experience, how important is it for women to support each other in the entrepreneurial space?**

Support among women in entrepreneurship is incredibly important. It's vital that we share not only the challenges we face but also the triumphs. By supporting one another, we can help each other navigate the complexities of business and life. Women have a unique ability to lift one another up and show each other a better way—both personally and professionally. When we collaborate, share knowledge, and celebrate each other's successes, we create a stronger, more empowering entrepreneurial community. It's about fostering a culture where women don't just survive, but thrive together.

Work-Life Balance & Self-Care

- **How do you maintain work-life balance while juggling the demands of entrepreneurship?**

Maintaining work-life balance is all about being intentional and purposeful in scheduling time off. As an entrepreneur, it's easy to get caught up in the constant demands of the business, but I've learned that taking time for myself, including vacations, is crucial for long-term success. I make sure to prioritize personal time just as much as I prioritize work, ensuring that I can recharge and return with renewed energy. By scheduling breaks and stepping away from work, I'm able to maintain focus, stay motivated, and avoid burnout. It's a constant balancing act, but I've learned that taking time for rest makes me more effective in my business and personal life.

- **What's your daily routine, and how do you incorporate self-care or downtime into your busy schedule?**

My schedule is definitely packed, but when I do have a moment of downtime, I like to stay connected with current events. I'll often scroll through my phone to catch up on the news—it's a simple way for me to stay informed and take a mental break from the day's demands.

- **What advice would you give to other women entrepreneurs who feel like they're burning out?**

My advice is simple: seek inner peace. When you're feeling burnt out, it's important to take a step back and center yourself. I rely on prayer and meditation to help me reconnect with my purpose and find clarity. These moments of quiet reflection allow me to reset mentally, emotionally, and spiritually. It's crucial to remember that you can't pour from an empty cup—taking the time to recharge is not only essential for your well-being but also for the health of your business. Don't be afraid to slow down and give yourself the space to breathe.

Innovation & Vision

- **How do you stay innovative and creative in a competitive market?**

Staying innovative in a competitive market requires a commitment to continuous education. I regularly read journals and keep up with the latest trends and developments in aesthetic medicine and technology. Staying informed about new devices and treatments allows me to offer cutting-edge services to my patients. But it's not just about my own education—I also prioritize educating my staff. By keeping the entire team informed and trained on the latest advancements, we ensure that Visage Laser & Skin Care remains at the forefront of the industry, providing top-quality care and innovative treatments to our clients.

- **What's the biggest risk you've ever taken in your business, and how did it pay off?**

The biggest risk I take is investing in advanced, non-invasive technologies for Visage Laser & Skin Care. These devices can be costly, and the market is highly competitive. However, I know that by offering state-of-the-art treatments, I set Visage apart and provide exceptional results that keep my patients coming back. This investment allows us to stay ahead of the curve, attract new clients, and strengthen our reputation as one of the leading medspas in the region. It's a calculated risk that continues to pay off by helping us grow and innovate in an ever-evolving industry.

- **What is your vision for the future of your business, and what steps are you taking to get there?**

My vision for the future of Visage Laser & Skin Care is for the business to eventually run independently, allowing me to step back from the day-to-day operations. I want to focus more on spending quality time with my family, especially my grandkids, and take the opportunity to travel and enjoy life outside of work. To get there, I'm actively building a strong, capable team and empowering them to take on more leadership responsibilities. I'm also refining our processes and systems to ensure that everything functions smoothly, even when I'm not as involved. This transition is all about creating a sustainable business that continues to thrive while giving me the time and freedom to enjoy other aspects of life.

Networking & Mentorship

- **Do you have a mentor, and if so, how has that relationship impacted your journey?**

I've had the privilege of having mentors throughout my career, and their guidance played a crucial role in shaping my journey. They provided invaluable advice, perspective, and support, especially during the early stages of my entrepreneurial path. However, nowadays, I find myself more in the position of being a mentor to others. I believe in giving back and sharing the knowledge and experiences I've gained, not just in the professional realm but also in personal development. By mentoring others, I can help guide and inspire the next generation of entrepreneurs, both professionally and personally. It's incredibly fulfilling to be able to pay it forward and contribute to the growth of others in all aspects of their lives.

- **What role has networking played in the success of your business?**

Networking has been crucial to the success of Visage Laser & Skin Care, but I rely on my team to actively build and foster connections with other businesses, entrepreneurs, and city officials. While I don't always initiate these connections, my staff plays an integral role in creating opportunities for collaboration and partnership. For example, through networking efforts, we've been able to expand our reach and strengthen our presence in the community. A recent highlight was my recognition as 2025 Woman of Distinction by Senator Steven Choi, which was a result of the relationships and networking we've built over time. Once connections are made, I take the opportunity to engage personally, ensuring that our business continues to grow through meaningful, impactful relationships with both individuals and organizations.

Impact and Legacy

- **What legacy do you want to leave behind for future generations of women entrepreneurs?**

I want to leave a legacy of integrity and honesty. I believe that women entrepreneurs should always strive to do the right thing, even when it's difficult. It's easy to get caught up in shortcuts or temporary gains, but true success comes from building a business with strong values. I hope to inspire future generations of women to lead with authenticity, maintain their principles, and build businesses that not only thrive but also make a positive impact on their communities. By doing so, they'll create lasting legacies of their own.

- **How does your business reflect your values and mission to empower other women?**

Visage Laser & Skin Care reflects my values of empowerment, integrity, and commitment to excellence. I strive to create an environment where women can feel confident, not only in their appearance but also in their ability to succeed. By offering non-invasive treatments that enhance their natural beauty, I empower my clients to feel better about themselves and to embrace their strengths. Additionally, I prioritize creating opportunities for women within my team, fostering a workplace where they can thrive professionally and personally. My mission is to help women feel confident and capable, both inside and out, while upholding values that support growth, respect, and success.

- **Have you used your platform to advocate for any social or political causes?**

Yes, I've used my platform to advocate for causes that are deeply important to me. As an immigrant who came to the U.S. seeking better opportunities, I understand firsthand the struggles and challenges that come with navigating the legal immigration system. I'm passionate about advocating for legal immigration for those seeking a new life here. I believe everyone deserves the chance to pursue their dreams, and I am committed to standing up for those in pursuit of a better future.

I'm also dedicated to supporting women who have endured trafficking. Through my work with a nonprofit organization, I've had the opportunity to donate treatments and help these women regain their confidence. One woman, in particular, came to me with severe acne that had deeply affected her self-esteem. After treating her, I saw her transformation—not just in her appearance, but in her renewed sense of self-worth. She went on to pursue a career as an electrician. These moments of empowerment drive me to continue supporting causes that make a real difference in people's lives.

In addition to these efforts, I actively donate and sponsor treatments to various organizations that help individuals in need, furthering my commitment to giving back and supporting those who could benefit most from aesthetic care.

Advice for Aspiring Entrepreneurs

- *What advice would you give to women who are thinking about starting their own business but are unsure?*

My advice is simple: stay optimistic, have hope, and be ready to work hard. It's important to dream big, but dreaming alone won't get you far. You need to roll up your sleeves, put in the work, and be willing to face challenges head-on.

- **What's the one thing you wish you had known before starting your business?**

The one thing I wish I had known is that it's harder than you think. No matter how much you plan or anticipate, there will always be unexpected challenges along the way. But despite the difficulties, it's absolutely worth it.

The rewards—both personally and professionally—make every challenge feel like a valuable lesson. Running a business requires perseverance, dedication, and the willingness to adapt, but the sense of accomplishment and the positive impact you can have on others make it all worthwhile.

- **What would you say to those who feel like they don't have the resources or support to launch their entrepreneurial dreams?**

I would say go about it the smart way—start with your business as a side hustle. Keep a steady income to cover your basic needs while you build the business. This way, you're not putting yourself under unnecessary pressure to make immediate profits. Entrepreneurship is a journey, and taking small, steady steps allows you to test the waters and learn along the way. If you try to jump in without a solid foundation, the risks can be overwhelming. Build your business carefully, and when the time is right, you can transition to full-time entrepreneurship with confidence.

Legacy and Giving Back

- **How do you give back to your community or industry through your business?**

Giving back is at the heart of everything I do. Whether it's sponsoring/donating treatments for individuals in need, mentoring women entrepreneurs, or supporting causes like human trafficking prevention, I use my platform to create meaningful change. My recognition as a **2025 Woman of Distinction by Senator Steven Choi** serves as a reminder that entrepreneurship is not just about personal success—it's about making a lasting impact on the community and paving the way for others to thrive. The legacy I want to leave is one where my contributions continue to inspire future generations of women to take bold steps, pursue their dreams, and uplift others along the way.

Website: www.visageskin.com

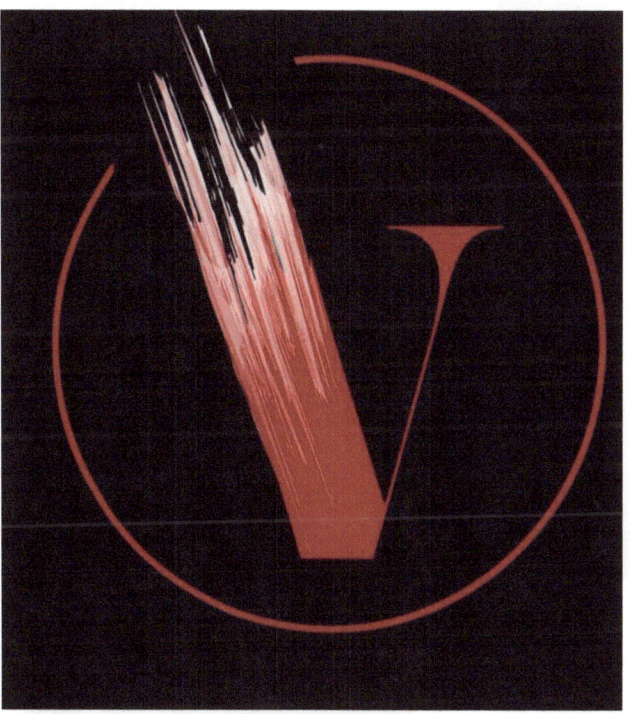

Connect With Dr. Katarzyna tesmer

www.visageskin.com

MEDICAL BILLING SUCCESS WITH CIARA & TARA

Join my partner Tara and I as we take Providers behind the scenes in Medical Billing and more.

Billing and credentialing are foundational pieces of your practice. If something goes wrong in either of these areas it can be an incredible headache to get it fixed. Even more than that, when your billing is incorrect, it's costing you money! If you're anything like the hundreds of clients we've worked with, billing is something you dread and keeps you worrying at night.

Now a **brand new podcast** focused on giving YOU the resources you need to work with insurance with confidence. We'll answer your biggest questions, give away our favorite tools, and provide all the insider information you need!

MONTHLY SUBSCRIPTION
www.talkbilling.info/offers/pzZjHHzz/checkout

BE A GUEST
www.talkbilling.info/offers/JB2eaaJz

YEARLY SUBSCRIPTION
www.talkbilling.info/offers/SSVRCLL5/checkout

BUY 1 EPISODE
www.talkbilling.info/store
www.ciara-lewis.mykajabi.com

CONTACT US FOR MORE DETAILS!

- klconsultingllc@gmail.com
- www.Klconsultllc.com
- www.ttmedbill.com
- Ciara Lewis
- Tara L Thomas
- @klconsultingllc

ENTREPRENEURSHIP, EMPOWERMENT, AND THE POWER OF ONE WOMAN'S YES

By Amy Chinian

Journey to Entrepreneurship

- **What was the moment or event that inspired you to start your entrepreneurial journey?**

Back in 2000, I was pregnant with my fifth child when my family went through a lice infestation. It was incredibly stressful, and to make matters worse, I couldn't find anything on the market that was both safe and effective. As a mom, I was frustrated and worried —nothing felt right for my kids. That's when the idea first started forming in my mind: there had to be a better way to help families going through this.

Fast forward a few years to 2007, during the recession—my husband's business collapsed, and suddenly, we had no stable income. With five kids depending on us, we needed a plan. I remembered our experience with lice and decided to take action. I put together a basket of non-toxic, carefully researched products and started offering in-home lice removal services. It started small, but word spread quickly. I think people appreciated the care and compassion I brought into their homes—and from there, My Hair Helpers was born. It's been an amazing journey, and I'm so grateful I get to help other families through something I once struggled with myself.

- **Were there any key challenges you faced early on, and how did you overcome them?**

With no marketing budget or prior business experience, I started small—offering in-home lice removal using a red picnic basket filled with non-toxic products I had carefully researched. The early days were tough. I made mistakes, from missing bugs to wrestling with long hair, but I refused to give up. By leading with kindness, compassion, and effective care, word of mouth slowly built a loyal community and a trusted reputation.

- **How did you transition from your previous career (if applicable) to being a full-time entrepreneur?**

At the time, I was a stay-at-home mom raising five kids while my husband ran a car business. Life was stable and comfortable—until a lice infestation hit our home when I was nine months pregnant with our fifth child. It was overwhelming and stressful, and trying to find professional help during that time was a challenge. That experience opened my eyes to a real need—and it ended up planting the seed for what would later become my business.

- **What were some unexpected hurdles you didn't anticipate when you first launched your business?**

One of the biggest challenges in growing a business is protecting your brand. It's so important to bring on people who truly respect what you've built and are committed to doing the work with integrity. Scaling means you can't do everything yourself—but the reality is, not everyone will stay loyal to your vision.

I've had employees who took what they learned from me and went on to start competing businesses. That was hard to process. But over time, I've learned to stay focused on what I'm building. Persistence, continuous learning, and taking small, intentional steps forward—that's what has helped me push through the setbacks and keep growing.

Empowerment & Resilience

- **What does being a 'fierce and fearless' woman entrepreneur mean to you personally?**

In business, things rarely go exactly as planned. For me, being fierce and fearless isn't about charging ahead blindly—it's about not being shaken by setbacks. When something doesn't work, I don't give up. I take a step back, reflect, pray, and look for another way forward.

I don't rush decisions—I stay strategic and thoughtful. Leading a business through tough times requires trust: trust that there are always answers, even if they're not obvious at first. You have to stay grounded, think creatively, and keep moving forward—one intentional step at a time.

- **How do you manage the balance between confidence and vulnerability in business?**

For me, it's about knowing who you can be vulnerable with. I've learned the hard way that being too open with the wrong people —especially in business—can lead to doubt or insecurity within your team. Vulnerability is important, but it needs to be shared wisely. That's why I reserve those honest moments for my inner circle —my husband and daughters—who I work closely with and trust completely. It's a balance: showing up as a confident leader while allowing yourself to be fully human behind the scenes, with the right support system in place.

- **Can you share a moment where you felt completely knocked down and how you managed to bounce back?**

In the early days of starting my business, there were plenty of moments that felt discouraging. My technique wasn't perfect, and I made mistakes. But instead of letting those setbacks define me, I saw them as signs that I needed to grow. I had to sharpen my skills, seek out education, and gain real experience.

I made a decision not to quit. I leaned into the learning process and let those challenges shape a better version of what I was building. That persistence—choosing to improve instead of walking away—is what allowed me to refine my approach and grow a much stronger business.

ENTREPRENEURSHIP, EMPOWERMENT, AND THE POWER OF ONE WOMAN'S YES

- **How do you maintain motivation during times of self-doubt or when facing criticism?**

For me, it all begins with how I start my day. I center myself through prayer and reading the Bible—it grounds me and helps me stay connected to my purpose. I remind myself why I do this work: to help families through a tough situation, to provide meaningful jobs for my team, and to support my own family. That purpose is what fuels me.

I also stay motivated by keeping a clear vision for the future—expanding our product line, opening more salons, and continuing to grow our nonprofit. Holding on to that bigger picture gives me the drive to keep going, even on the hardest days.

Leadership & Growth

- **What leadership qualities do you believe are essential for women in entrepreneurship?**

Integrity, compassion, and humor are at the core of how I lead. Stability and the ability to cast a clear, achievable vision are just as important. As a leader, it's not enough to know where you're headed—you have to bring your team along with you, inspire them, and offer support along the way.

And humor—especially in unconventional or high-stress situations—makes a big difference. A light heart and a good laugh can keep you grounded and help you connect with others, even in the middle of a crisis. It's one of the most underrated leadership tools.

- **How do you foster a culture of empowerment within your team or business?**

I foster a culture of empowerment through encouragement, support, and leading by example. Sometimes that means lightening the mood with laughter, but more often, it's about consistently reminding my team that they're doing a great job. I believe in pouring into them—not just professionally, but personally.

I share practical advice, like how to save and invest wisely, and I emphasize the value of a spiritual foundation and a well-balanced life. I do my best to live out what I teach—showing that it's possible to succeed in both family and business. I've raised five children, been married for 35 years, and I firmly believe in giving, not just taking—especially when it comes to lifting up others in need.

- **As your business has grown, what have you learned about the art of delegation?**

I've learned that no one excels at everything—and that's perfectly okay. Delegation is key. It's about bringing in people who are strong in areas where you may not be. I have a blog writer, an advertising expert, a graphic designer, and someone who manages my Amazon store. Each person plays a role in moving the business forward.

Building a solid team around you is essential. You can't do it all—and you definitely can't do it all well. Letting go and trusting others is one of the smartest things you can do as a business owner.

- **How do you prioritize your personal growth alongside the growth of your business?**

I prioritize personal growth by staying curious and committed to learning. I actively seek out mentors and pay close attention to successful businesses—I'm always studying what works and why. Everything is constantly evolving—the internet, how we market, how we reach customers—so it's important to stay up to date.

Being open to change and willing to adapt has helped me grow not just as a person but as a leader. It's what keeps my business moving forward.

Challenges Specific to Women Entrepreneurs

- **What do you think are some of the biggest challenges women face when starting a business, and how do you navigate them?**

One of the biggest challenges I've faced is having enough capital to start and grow a business without going into debt. I've learned to build gradually—reinvesting what comes in and being careful not to take on more than I can manage. I've also kept things close to home by partnering with my husband, rather than bringing in outside investors, which can often complicate things.

Another challenge has been visibility. There are so many successful women in business, but we don't hear their stories as often—men still dominate much of the spotlight. The truth is, women are incredible multitaskers and strong business leaders. We just need to keep telling our stories and lifting each other up.

- **Have you faced any gender-related biases in your career, and how did you respond to them?**

I believe I have, especially when men walk into one of my locations and hear my story. When I share how my husband's business collapsed and we had to start over—and that I stepped up, built this company from the ground up, and now he works alongside me—it often shifts their perspective. It challenges assumptions about who leads and who builds. Sharing that journey helps people see that women are not only capable of leading businesses, but of doing so in the face of real adversity—and thriving.

- **In your experience, how important is it for women to support each other in the entrepreneurial space?**

I think it's incredibly important. I love it when I meet another woman in business—there's a special camaraderie and understanding between us. Being an entrepreneur takes a unique kind of person: a risk-taker and an independent thinker. So, when we connect, it feels meaningful and energizing. I truly enjoy exchanging ideas and hearing their success stories. It's not only inspiring—it's a lot of fun, and I absolutely love it.

Work-Life Balance & Self-Care

- **How do you maintain work-life balance while juggling the demands of entrepreneurship?**

I maintain balance by surrounding myself with a talented team I trust to handle daily operations, which lets me focus on the bigger picture. Delegating is key to growing without burning out. My faith and sense of purpose keep me motivated, and I make sure to take time for self-care and recharge when needed. Remembering that the work is bigger than me—and that I have a supportive team—helps me stay grounded.

- **What's your daily routine, and how do you incorporate self-care or downtime into your busy schedule?**

I start my mornings at 7 a.m. with coffee, followed by daily devotion, Bible reading, and prayer. It grounds me and sets the tone for the day. Sometimes I'll even send a devotion to the women on my team—it's a simple way to uplift and stay connected with them.

After that, I dive into the day's responsibilities. I manage six salons remotely, handle inventory, create staff schedules, and address customer service needs. Every day looks a little different, but staying rooted in faith and purpose helps me navigate it all.

Despite the demands of running a business, I make self-care a priority. I go to the gym three times a week, take Pilates classes, and incorporate sauna sessions and red light therapy into my routine. Sundays are sacred—I go to church and catch up with friends over lunch. And my husband and I love dining out together—we make time for dinner dates four to five nights a week. It's all part of staying healthy, connected, and energized.

- **What advice would you give to other women entrepreneurs who feel like they're burning out?**

You have to carve out time for self-care a few times a week—it's not optional, it's essential. Whether it's a walk, some fresh air, or lunch with a friend, those moments help you reset. For me, I love going to my gym—it's an all-women's space that feels more like a spa. It's peaceful, uplifting, and a great way to connect with others.

Taking care of yourself isn't selfish—it's necessary. Because if you're not well, you can't show up fully for anyone else.

Innovation & Vision

- **How do you stay innovative and creative in a competitive market?**

I'm extremely competitive—it's just part of who I am. I was competitive in sports as a child, and now I bring that same drive into my business. I'm always learning, observing what others are doing, and figuring out the best ways to serve my customers. If I'm going to do something, I want to be the best at it. That mindset keeps me pushing forward, staying creative, and continually raising the bar.

- **What's the biggest risk you've ever taken in your business, and how did it pay off?**

I think the biggest risk I ever took was finding the confidence to open my first physical location. For 15 years, I had been going house to house with my products and services, so making the decision to invest in a brick-and-mortar space was a major leap. But it turned out to be the right one. That first location did so well, I was able to open five more. Taking that risk was scary—but absolutely worth it.

- **What is your vision for the future of your business, and what steps are you taking to get there?**

My vision is to take my products, services, and nonprofit work nationwide. Every day, I'm moving toward that goal—opening new locations and refining our product line. I want families to be able to easily purchase our products across multiple platforms and access clear, step-by-step instructional videos.

Lice removal isn't as simple as people think, and too often, parents turn to harsh chemicals out of desperation. That concerns me deeply. I'm committed to expanding access to safe, effective solutions—so families everywhere can get the help they need without compromising their health.

Networking & Mentorship

- **Do you have a mentor, and if so, how has that relationship impacted your journey?**

Yes—my husband has absolutely been my mentor. He built a multimillion-dollar company from the ground up and spent 40 years in the car business. Even though he lost everything during the 2008 recession, he never lost his wisdom or entrepreneurial spirit.

He's been by my side every step of the way, offering guidance, encouragement, and perspective. His resilience and support have been a constant source of inspiration throughout my journey.

- **What role has networking played in the success of your business?**

Networking has been absolutely crucial. You have to know exactly who your target audience is and be intentional about where you invest your time. For me, that means building relationships with schools, school nurses, pediatricians, teachers, and even Facebook parenting groups—those are my key networks.

It's all about focusing your energy where it matters most and connecting with the right people who can help you grow your business in a meaningful way.

- **How do you foster strong, supportive relationships with other entrepreneurs?**

I build strong relationships by being open and transparent—sharing what's worked for me and, just as importantly, what hasn't. I always try to help others in areas where I've found success, especially if they're facing challenges I've already navigated.

To me, it's about reaching out and saying, "This worked for me—maybe it can help you too." Supporting one another through the ups and downs is what makes this journey more meaningful.

Impact and Legacy

- **What legacy do you want to leave behind for future generations of women entrepreneurs?**

I want my story to show that it's possible to start from nothing and still overcome enormous challenges. We weren't just low on funds—we were a million dollars in debt after my husband's company collapsed. But I stayed focused on my vision and took it one step at a time. I didn't let the weight of it all paralyze me.

Having a clear purpose was what kept me going. And part of that purpose is creating a legacy—helping children who face the unique challenge of head lice. No child should have to suffer or have their confidence and childhood defined by something so treatable. That's what drives me every day.

- **How does your business reflect your values and mission to empower other women?**

My business is built on compassion and a genuine desire to help others. The challenges my family and I have faced have shaped me and given me a deep empathy for people going through similar struggles. That desire to support and serve is at the core of everything I do.

I also encourage other entrepreneurs to find a niche they truly love—and then commit to being the best at it. Mediocrity isn't enough. When you strive for excellence, your value rises, and people take notice. That's how you create real impact—and that's where true empowerment begins.

Advice for Aspiring Entrepreneurs

- **What advice would you give to women who are thinking about starting their own business but are unsure?**

It really comes down to finding something you're great at—and then doing your homework. Study your competition. Take what works, leave what doesn't, and put your own unique, creative spin on it. Start small and build gradually. There's no need to take on a huge loan right away and get buried in debt. I began by going door to door, offering services until I had the customer base to support opening a salon.

Hiring the right people is also key. You need loyal, trustworthy team members because you can't grow alone. As my business expanded, I brought on others to cover new areas and eventually added specialists like a Google Ads expert and a publicist. Growth doesn't have to be fast to be successful—sometimes the slow, steady path is the most sustainable.

- **What's the one thing you wish you had known before starting your business?**

One of the biggest lessons I've learned is that people aren't always who they appear to be. In business, you have to be careful not to be overly trusting—even with those who seem like friends. I've had a few painful experiences where women I had helped significantly, both financially and personally, later used what they learned from me to start their own competing businesses.

It was a tough and surprising reality. Sometimes, the people who seemed the kindest—or needed the most support—turned out not to have the best intentions. It taught me to be more guarded, while still leading with compassion. You can be generous, but you also have to protect what you've built.

- **What would you say to those who feel like they don't have the resources or support to launch their entrepreneurial dreams?**

Don't despise small beginnings. Focus on fine-tuning your craft—whatever it is. If that means working for someone else to gain experience and improve your skills, that's okay. Most people need time in the field before they're truly ready to branch out on their own.

It's all part of the process. Every opportunity is a chance to learn, grow, and prepare for what's next. Embrace that season and trust that, when the time is right, you'll be ready to build something of your own.

Legacy and Giving Back

- **How do you give back to your community or industry through your business?**

I give back by sending products to orphanages and supporting underserved communities in Mexico. I've personally traveled there with supplies, teaching women how to safely remove lice—because in many of the places I visited, nearly 90% of the people were affected.

I never turn anyone away because of money. I truly believe this work is something God has called me to do. If I can help restore a child's confidence, improve their self-image, and allow them to reconnect socially—so they can simply enjoy being a kid without worrying about lice—that's what drives me every day.

- **What role does philanthropy play in your entrepreneurial journey?**

Philanthropy plays a central role in my entrepreneurial journey—it's not something I do on the side; it's woven into the heart of my mission. As I grow my business, I'm equally focused on giving back through my nonprofit, *Lice Free Forever*. We provide lice treatment products and education to underserved communities, especially in areas like Mexico, where access is limited and the need is overwhelming.

I've personally traveled to deliver supplies and train women, often finding that entire communities are struggling with this issue. I never turn anyone away because of money. I believe God always provides, so I focus on serving with compassion and purpose. For me, success isn't just about profit—it's about impact.

- **Website:** www.myhairhelpers.com

FIERCE & FEARLESS ENTREPRENEUR: DR. TYWANNA SMITH

Identity & Origin

- **What does being "fierce and fearless" mean to you, and how has that shown up in your life?**

Being "fierce and fearless" means being confident and bold. It's about not being afraid to pivot when life calls for it, and showing up fully as yourself—with no reservations. I've had to embody that mindset both as a mother and as a woman in sports, consistently showing up, pushing through, and leading with authenticity every single day.

- **Take us back—what moment ignited your entrepreneurial journey?**

I get my entrepreneurial spirit from my father. He was a blue-collar worker who didn't have much in terms of material wealth, but what he did have was grit. Even through sickness, I watched him rise every day to run his own auto repair shop—committed to providing for my sister and me. That kind of courage left a mark on me.

I first put that courage into action when I became a financial advisor at Merrill Lynch. Working with professional athletes, I quickly saw that their needs went far beyond traditional financial planning. They needed deeper support, more education, and strategic guidance for life both during and after sports. That realization inspired me to launch my own firm—one that could serve the full spectrum of their complex, evolving needs.

- **Did you always see yourself as a leader, or did that identity evolve over time?**

I've always seen myself as a leader—something my mom helped instill in me early on. She used to tell me I was the "total package," and that confidence stuck. Being tall meant I often stood out, and naturally, people looked to me for direction. Over time, that constant expectation helped me grow more comfortable taking charge and trusting my voice. While leadership was always there, it definitely evolved as I stepped into more roles that required decisive action and responsibility.

- **What personal values do you refuse to compromise on in your business?**

I I will never compromise my integrity. I believe in letting results speak for themselves—and in winning the right way. I also refuse to compromise on being a mother first. Too often, motherhood is seen as a limitation in business, as if it somehow lessens our ability to deliver. But I see it as a strength. I want to be fully present for the important moments in my children's lives, and I'm grateful that entrepreneurship gives me the flexibility to do just that.

Business Building

- **What was the most unexpected lesson you learned while building your business?**

I learned that you can be the best choice for an opportunity—and still not be chosen. That was an unexpected and tough lesson. It taught me to shift my focus to what I can control. Every "no" simply brings me one step closer to the right "yes." That's where I choose to put my energy.

- **Have you ever wanted to quit? What made you stay in the game?**

II won't say I've ever wanted to quit—because quitting wasn't something my parents ever instilled in me. But I have definitely felt the need to pivot, especially when my work began to conflict with my priorities around family. During COVID, I deeply questioned whether I was still called to this work. But every time I've reached that point, God has opened the door to something even bigger. That's what keeps me in the game.

- **How do you define success on your own terms?**

Success is often measured by outcomes, but I believe the internal markers matter just as much. For me, success means having peace and a sense of purpose in the work I do—especially when it impacts the lives of others. True success is both personal and meaningful.

- **What mindset shift changed everything for you as an entrepreneur?**

After I became a mom, I had to learn how to juggle it all—and it wasn't easy. But in many ways, motherhood made me a better sports advisor and entrepreneur. It taught me to be a stronger planner, a more intentional listener, and a sharper problem-solver for my clients. That heightened sense of attentiveness directly enhanced how I serve my athletes.

- **What is one mistake that taught you more than any win ever could?**

One mistake I made early in my career was trying to be someone I wasn't. I showed up as who I thought a financial advisor should be, instead of just being myself. Over time, I realized that it's your authenticity that truly resonates with people.

- **If you could write a letter to your Day 1 self, what would it say?**

Be yourself and enjoy the ride! Too often, we hold back joy, waiting for the "right" moment or perfect conditions. But life is happening now—dance in the rain, take the trip, celebrate the small wins. The journey is worth it, and you can succeed while fully embracing each step along the way.

Resilience & Mental Wellness

- **How do you protect your peace while pursuing big goals?**

IIn sports terms, sometimes you have to take a timeout! I intentionally disconnect and lean into time with my children and family. It's how I prevent burnout and stay grounded. Traveling with them is my reset—it keeps me energized, balanced, and ready to show up fully for the goals I'm pursuing.

- **How do you bounce back when life knocks you off course?**

I pray. I fast. I spend more time with God. This has been the single most impactful practice in my life that has allowed me to keep growing and remain resilient when facing adversity. My faith is my rock and cheat code.

- **What role does self-care play in your success—and what does it look like for you?**

Self-care is vital to sustainable success. Notice I didn't just say "success"—anyone can win for a season. But to keep winning, consistently and over time, you have to invest in yourself. I prioritize travel, quiet time at home, and reading. I've learned we're not machines—we have to nourish our mind, body, and soul if we want to experience long-term success.

- **How do you separate self-worth from your business performance?**

This is hard! I've learned that there are many things outside of my control. However, if I do my best, more often than not, I'll see the results I'm looking for. When you chase performance alone, you're tempted to cut corners. But when you focus on becoming your best self, fulfillment follows.

Feminine Leadership & Impact

- **Do you think women lead differently—and if so, how has that shaped your leadership style?**

Yes, I believe women lead differently. We're strategic thinkers who lead with both strength and empathy. We care deeply—and that matters when you're working with people. That awareness has shaped my leadership style. It's made me a more thoughtful listener and a more intentional, decisive leader. One often-overlooked aspect of leadership is truly understanding the needs and challenges of those you lead. That's how you create real impact.

- **How do you handle being underestimated or misjudged in a male-dominated space?**

In male-dominated spaces, I've learned not to let misconceptions push me into overcompensating or showing up aggressively. Instead, I focus inward—on my gifts, my purpose, and how I can lead through service. How can I elevate the room? How can I make someone better? When I stay grounded in my calling and pour into those who are ready to receive it, external barriers become background noise.

- **What legacy do you want to leave for women who come after you?**

I want the women who come after me to know that they can pursue greatness in any field—including sports—and do it without compromising who they are. You can lead with grace, a nurturing spirit, and bold conviction. The lane is wide enough for you to be powerful and authentic.

- **What do you wish more women would say to each other in business?**

"You're doing a great job." I wish more women said that to each other in business. Affirmation goes a long way—being seen builds confidence, and confidence inspires action. We need more encouragement, more support, and more celebration of one another. We truly need each other.

Vision & Purpose

- **What's next for you—and what impact do you hope to create?**

I'm focused on continuing to build a global network for athletes competing internationally. Through the expansion of the Athletes Abroad Summit, I want to create a world-class experience that delivers education, resources, and powerful connections for American athletes playing overseas. I'm also passionate about equipping the next generation with financial tools early on. My goal is to bring my signature curriculum, Teen Money Box, to teens around the world—and help them build strong financial foundations that will last a lifetime.

If your brand had a message for every woman reading this right now, what would it be?

Know yourself—and choose what brings you peace. If something doesn't allow you to live in your purpose or share your gifts with the world, it might not be for you. And that's okay. Give yourself permission to live freely, stand in your truth, and do good for others along the way.

Connect With Dr. Tywanna Smith

Website: www.tywannasmith.com
Instagram: @drtywannasmith
LinkedIn: Dr. Tywanna Smith

THRIVING IN THE GREY: THE REALITY OF BEING A DISABLED BUSINESSWOMAN WITH CHRONIC ILLNESS

By Andrea Cennington, MSW, LCSW, LCSW-C, LICSW, QS

Running a business is often romanticized as a fast-paced, glamorous life filled with boardroom deals, networking mixers, and non-stop productivity. But for those of us living with chronic illness and disability, entrepreneurship looks radically different—and profoundly powerful in its own right.

I'm a businesswoman who lives daily with invisible illnesses that don't clock out. Pain, fatigue, brain fog, mobility issues, and flare-ups are not footnotes—they're co-workers in my entrepreneurial journey. Yet, despite these challenges, I run my business with pride, integrity, and a pace that honors my body and boundaries.

Navigating Entrepreneurship with a Chronic Illness

Let me be clear: chronic illness doesn't diminish ambition. If anything, it intensifies it. It requires ingenuity, discipline, and a deep well of inner resilience. Being a disabled entrepreneur means learning to adapt not only my business model, but my entire mindset around success.

Gone are the 80-hour workweeks. Gone is the illusion that hustle equals worth. I have had to redefine productivity in a way that centers sustainability, rest, and radical self-compassion. I learned to structure my business around my life—not the other way around.

The Isolation and Invisibility

One of the most misunderstood aspects of being a disabled businesswoman is the invisibility. If you don't "look sick," people assume you're fine. If you take a day off to manage symptoms, others might question your work ethic. But what they don't see is the emotional calculus we make each morning—deciding whether today is a day for grinding or simply surviving.

This invisibility can also extend into entrepreneurial spaces. Networking events rarely accommodate mobility, sensory, or energy limitations. Speaking engagements often require travel and exposure to environmental stressors. Even virtual spaces can be overwhelming for those with cognitive challenges.

Yet, we show up. Often without applause or acknowledgment. We build, create, and lead—even as we privately nurse flares, adjust medication, or excuse ourselves to rest.

Building a Business on My Terms

Owning my business has been one of the most liberating decisions of my life. It gave me what so many workplaces failed to offer: flexibility, dignity, and alignment. I built a trauma-informed, healing-centered practice because I knew what it felt like to be overlooked, misjudged, and minimized. And I wasn't going to replicate that harm.

Being both a clinician and a CEO means I get to hire differently, lead with empathy, and create systems that leave room for humanity. My chronic illness doesn't weaken my leadership—it

Lessons I've Learned Along the Way

1. *Rest is resistance:* In a culture obsessed with output, choosing to rest is revolutionary.
2. *Boundaries are life-saving:* Not every opportunity is worth your health.
3. *Accessibility is not optional:* It's a moral and practical imperative—for yourself and others.
4. *Asking for help is a power move:* Delegating and outsourcing are survival tools, not signs of failure.
5. *You're not an inspiration for existing:* You are a skilled, capable, visionary leader—your disability doesn't disqualify that.

To My Fellow Disabled Entrepreneurs

Your journey is valid. Your pace is enough. Your business is worthy. You don't need to over-explain your pain or apologize for your limitations. You're allowed to thrive in a different rhythm.
May we build businesses that don't exploit us—and legacies that honor our healing.

Andrea Cennington is the founder and clinical director of *Bloomed Within, LLC*, a trauma-informed mental health practice rooted in healing, equity, and sustainable success. She is also a proud disabled veteran, author, and survivor using her voice to challenge systems and inspire change.

WRITE THE BOOK.
BUILD THE LEGACY.

We empower Christian authors to self-publish without losing their voice or values.

- Book Coaching & Editing
- Cover & Interior Design
- Launch Strategy & Marketing
- Custom Merch & Websites
- Post-Launch Support & Coaching

📞 **660.221.3370**

🌐 **marilynjeannedesigns.com**

Gina Stockdall
CEO & Founder

THE BALANCED HUSTLE: NAVIGATING LIFE AS A WOMAN ENTREPRENEUR

By Chinyere Iroanya

Finding Balance: A Real Talk on Work-Life Harmony for Women Entrepreneurs

Hey there, fellow hustlers! Let's chat about something that often feels like trying to catch smoke with your bare hands: work-life balance. As a woman entrepreneur juggling a million tasks, I know firsthand how tricky it can be to keep everything in harmony. So, grab your favorite drink, and let's dive into how I navigate this wild ride, my daily routine, and some real advice for anyone feeling the burnout creep in.

The Morning Magic: Setting the Tone

My day kicks off around 6:00 AM, but let's be real—sometimes it's more like 6:30 AM (thanks, snooze button!). I start with a little "me time"—a mix of meditation and just soaking in the quiet. If you are a "Yogite" (I just made this up to define someone who does Yoga), then that may be the time to bring out your mat and spread it! And if you are all for early breakfasts, a warm cup of tea or coffee can do some magic (nope, it's too early for me, so I pass). This morning magic sets a positive vibe, and trust me, it makes all the difference.

By 7:00 AM, I join an online prayer line for the next one and a half hours (but when I have to do other things while at it, I still do what I have to do while praying). It's a powerful spiritual exercise that gets me all charged up. Then, I dive into work! I tackle my hardest tasks first because, let's face it, my brain is still fresh and ready to roll. I'm all about time-blocking, which helps me stay focused (mostly). But life happens, and when inspiration strikes or a curveball comes my way, I adapt. Flexibility is key!

Self-Care: Little Moments Count

Now, here's where it gets real. As entrepreneurs, self-care often gets pushed to the back burner. But I'm learning to make a big deal of it, even if it's just a few minutes here and there. I take short breaks to stretch, breathe, or even dance it out to my favorite song. Yes, I'm that person in the office! And if this doesn't work for you, how about you learn to work while standing, play a silly game on your phone, compete against your last score, or watch a comedy skit or something that is not work-related? I find this therapeutic.

Lunchtime is my sacred escape. I step away from my desk and enjoy a meal without scrolling through emails. Whether it's a lunch date with friends or a solo coffee shop visit, these moments recharge my spirit.

I wrap up my workday by 5:00 PM, which feels like a small victory, but it's done with intentionality. Whether I'm cooking something or catching up on my latest Netflix obsession, that downtime is crucial for my sanity.

Boundaries: Your Best Friend

One of the biggest lessons I've learned is the power of boundaries. It's easy to feel like you need to be available 24/7, but that's a recipe for burnout. I've started setting clear work hours and sticking to them. Trust me, it's okay to say no! This shift not only helps me respect my time but also allows me to show up fully in both my personal and professional lives. Meet, right?

Real Talk: Tips to Beat Burnout

To all my fellow women entrepreneurs out there—if you're feeling overwhelmed, you're in good company. Here's some friendly advice that's helped me along the way:

Tune In to Your Body: If you're feeling drained, listen up! Taking a break isn't a sign of weakness; it's a smart move for long-term success. Easier said than done when you have deadlines to meet, right? How about you take an early break when your body says so and then steal some time from your rest-time block to make it up? After all, you rested earlier—it's payback time. And nope, it's not a habit; it just so happened.

Get Support: Don't do it all alone. Build a support network and delegate tasks that drain your energy. Teamwork makes the dream work! It's not just a slogan but a life-saving hack. Buy back your time, energy, and focus by delegating any distractions.

Focus on What Matters: Spend time on activities that align with your passions and goals. It's totally okay to pass on opportunities that don't excite you; it saves you energy for what really matters. After all, fulfilling your purpose is the goal, and that shouldn't hurt your sanity.

Celebrate the Wins: This sounds cliché, I know, but committing to celebrating your achievements—big or small—is real self-motivation! Recognizing progress boosts your mood. Be your own greatest cheerleader because only you know what you've had to overcome to achieve that seemingly small feat that others tend to trivialize.

Make Self-Care Non-Negotiable: Whether it's a bubble bath, a walk in nature, or indulging in your favorite hobby, prioritize those feel-good activities. They grease your brain and body wheels and make you function optimally!

Finally: Embrace the Journey

Finding balance is about making choices that work for you. By incorporating self-care into my daily routine, setting boundaries, and listening to my needs, I'm slowly but surely creating a life that feels good—both professionally and personally.

So, to all the incredible women out there hustling on all fronts—as CEOs of your lives and homes, you deserve success and serenity. Remember, balance is within reach—it just takes a little practice and a lot of self-love. Let's support each other in this beautiful chaos of entrepreneurship!

BEYOND THE PAPER: HOW ONE COACH HELPS PARENTS USE THE IEP AS A ROADMAP TO ADULTHOOD

By: Susan Tatem, Founder of Bright Path Coaching

When my daughter was first placed on an IEP, I thought it was just about helping her get through school. I know how overwhelming and intimidating these meetings can be. As a coach for families raising children with autism, I quickly realized this document had the power to shape her future far beyond academics. But here's what I want every parent to know: you have all the power! You are not at the mercy of the system. You have the legal rights, the insight, and the final say. An IEP isn't just a piece of paper—it's a tool that, when done right, can help prepare your child not just for graduation, but for life.

One of the biggest mistakes I see parents make when it comes to IEP meetings is walking in without a vision. Before you even sit down at that table, ask yourself: Where do I want my child to be in five or ten years? Your answer should shape every goal, support, and service discussed in that meeting. A strong IEP isn't just about academics—it's about life. That means requesting goals that build functional, real-world skills like job readiness, time management, communication, self-advocacy, and emotional regulation. Don't wait until high school to start. You don't have to have all the answers today, but start asking the right questions. By middle school, your child's IEP can and should include transition goals that begin moving them toward greater independence.

Be intentional about using strengths-based language in the goals, and don't be afraid to rewrite them if they sound limiting or vague. Words matter. Most importantly, remember this: you have the right to ask questions, make suggestions, and say "no." You are not there to rubber-stamp the school's plan—you're there to collaborate. A respectful partnership is best, but don't shy away from speaking up. You know your child better than anyone, and you have every right to shape their path forward.

IEP meetings can feel intimidating, especially when you're sitting at a table full of professionals. But remember: you are the most important member of the team. Your child has rights under the law. Come prepared. Bring a written list of your child's strengths, challenges, goals, and any concerns you want addressed. It's okay to ask for clarification, to question recommendations, or to take time before agreeing to changes. Stay focused on the big picture: How does this IEP support my child's long-term success? Push for meaningful, measurable goals that align with their future—not just what's convenient for the school! Take notes, keep a journal of events (including dates, times, and names), always follow up in writing, and know that you can call a meeting at any time. Your voice matters. Don't be afraid to use it.

High school isn't the finish line—it's the launchpad. By the time your child enters ninth grade, the focus should have shifted from surviving the school day to preparing for adult life. That means building skills both inside and outside the classroom. Think beyond academics: Can they manage their time? Manage money? Navigate a schedule? Communicate their needs? Follow through on tasks without constant prompting?

Every IEP goal should point toward greater independence. Push for goals that target daily living skills, problem-solving, emotional regulation, and social communication. If your child struggles with executive functioning, for example, ask for support in areas like planning ahead, completing multi-step tasks, or organizing materials.

Research and pursue real-world experiences. Many schools offer work-based learning, internships, or job-shadowing opportunities. Find out about community partnerships, supported employment options, and volunteer opportunities. Even basic responsibilities at home—doing laundry, budgeting, cooking—can be written into IEP goals to strengthen life readiness. Knowledge is power. The earlier you begin preparing, the smoother the transition into adulthood will be—for both you and your child.

The law requires a transition plan to be part of your child's IEP by age 16, but I always encourage families to start by 12 if possible. Why? Because planning early gives your child more time to explore, build confidence, and develop the skills they'll need after graduation.

A strong transition plan isn't just a checkbox—it's a roadmap. It should reflect your child's interests, strengths, and long-term goals. Whether your child is headed toward college, trade school, supported employment, or day programs, the IEP should outline specific steps to help them move in that direction. This phase is about preparing, not pressuring. Some kids thrive in structured programs; others need flexibility and creativity. And that's okay. An IEP is a living, breathing document and should depict where your child is now and where they are heading. It's okay if plans change, but you always want to see this basic pattern in place. The goal isn't to map out every step to adulthood overnight—it's to make sure your child isn't standing at the edge of graduation wondering, Now what?

If you're feeling worried, unsure, or overwhelmed, take heart—you're not alone. You don't have to figure it all out today, but every step you take now makes a difference later. I've been in your shoes. That's why I created Bright Path Coaching. I walk the trenches alongside families like yours and help you build a clear, personalized roadmap for the teen years and beyond. I help parents shift from overwhelm to clarity, fear to peace of mind, isolated to empowered. Together, we clarify the vision for your child's future, break big goals into manageable steps, and make sure you're never walking this journey alone. With the right support, your child's path can be bright, full of possibility, and lead to an independent, fulfilling adult life.

Let's build their bright path—one confident step at a time.

Connect With Susan Tatem

Facebook.com/SusanMTatem
brightpath4autism.org
www.linkedin.com/in/susan-tatem-brightpath
brightpath4autism@gmail.com

Bright Path Coaching

From Uncertainty to Clarity, Confidence, and a Plan: Helping Parents Build Brighter Futures for Teens with Autism

Take the first step toward a brighter future.

1 ON 1 COACHING

VIP POWER HOUR

GROUP CALLS

SUPPORT COMMUNITY

AND MORE!

Susan Tatem
Founder, CEO, TVHost,
Bestseling Author

brightpath4atuism.org

brightpath4autism@gmail.com; 804-577-8878

FINDING YOUR POWER AND BEAUTY AFTER TRAUMA

By Sonia Rodrigues, Psychotherapist and Founder of Transition to Wellness

If you've been through trauma, you know how disorienting it can feel. Suddenly, the world no longer makes sense. Who you were before the pain may feel like a distant memory, and who you are now might feel like someone you don't quite recognize. As a psychotherapist who has spent over 25 years walking beside women through their healing journeys, I want you to know this: your story does not end in the moment you were hurt. In fact, something incredibly powerful can begin right there—a moment where you can revive your power and your beauty.

Healing from trauma isn't about erasing the pain. It's about learning how to live in a new way—one that honors what you've been through while helping you reconnect with your strength, your voice, and your beauty.

The Myth of Brokenness

So many women come to me believing they are broken. Trauma has a way of convincing us that we are too damaged to move forward. But here's the truth: you are not broken—you are wounded, and wounds can heal. In the process of that healing, you may even discover parts of yourself that are stronger, wiser, and more deeply alive than ever before.

There is beauty in your courage. There is power in your survival. And there is lots of possibility in your future.

Reclaiming Your Power

After trauma, it's common to feel powerless. Something happened that you didn't choose, that you couldn't control. But reclaiming your power doesn't mean pretending everything is okay. It means learning to listen to your needs, set boundaries, speak your truth, and make choices that reflect your worth.

Power doesn't always roar. Sometimes it whispers and sounds like this: "I'm allowed to rest." Or, "I don't have to do this all at once." Or, "I matter."

Every time you choose to care for yourself, to ask for help, or to say no, you are stepping back into your power.

Recognizing Your Beauty

There's a quiet kind of beauty that emerges from women who have done the hard work of healing. It's not always visible on the outside, but it radiates from within. It's the beauty of a woman who has learned to trust herself again. A woman who carries her scars with dignity and softness. A woman who knows her worth not because someone told her, but because she claimed it for herself.

Beauty after trauma is not about perfection. It's about presence. It's about living from a place of authenticity, vulnerability, and strength.

Finding the Right Support

Healing doesn't happen in isolation. Don't try to do it all on your own; find the right supports and connect with people who will support you and help you rise above. One of the reasons why I created Transition to Wellness was to create a space for women to feel supported, empowered, and understood as they move through trauma and into a new chapter of life. Together, we work to rebuild a sense of safety, clarity, and purpose. You don't need to have all the answers. You just need a safe place to begin.

The Next Chapter

Your pain is part of your story, but it is not the whole story. The next chapter is yours to write—and it can be one of power, beauty, and wholeness. Even now, especially now, you are building upon who you were and creating a new chapter for yourself, stronger and more resilient than before.

And that, in itself, is something truly beautiful.

Connect With Sonia Rodrigues

www.transitiontowellness.com
nstagram: transition.to.wellness

BEYOND BURNOUT: SELF-CARE FOR THE WOMAN WHO DOES IT ALL

By Lakeisha Lee

Self-Care for Professionals

Kyleah, my brilliant child, once asked me, "What did you lose when there was nothing to gain?"

At first, I didn't know how to answer. But after sitting with her words, I realized this wasn't just a question—it was a mirror. So often, we hold onto situations, people, and habits that no longer serve us. We stay connected out of fear, routine, or the illusion that we're gaining something. But what if, in truth, we're just afraid to let go?

That one question sparked a deep reflection—not just as a mother, but as a professional, a leader, and a woman who had to learn how to care for others and herself. It reminded me that self-reflection and self-care aren't extras. They're essential.

The Fear of Losing

Most of us aren't taught how to lose. We're raised to win—to work harder, aim higher, prove others wrong. We're praised for pushing through, even when we're breaking inside. But that mindset can trap us. We start clinging to people, routines, or roles, not because they help us grow, but because they're familiar.

Even our exhaustion becomes a pattern.

And yet, some of the most powerful growth happens when we release what no longer fits. Letting go isn't weakness—it's strength. And sometimes, it's the only way we can move forward.

Recognizing Unhealthy Patterns

Unhealthy patterns aren't always loud. They often look like "just getting through the day." As educators, leaders, and caregivers, we tend to run on autopilot, convincing ourselves that burnout is normal.

It's not.

We keep chasing results, staying busy, and ignoring our own needs—until we can't anymore. That's why reflection matters. If we don't pause to check in with ourselves, we end up stuck in cycles that steal our peace.

Ask yourself:

- What habits feel draining instead of nourishing?
- What are you doing out of guilt instead of alignment?
- Are your "yeses" rooted in purpose—or in fear?

We can't change what we don't name.

People, Expectations, and Experiences

Some of the hardest things to release are people and expectations. But not everything or everyone is meant to come with us. Some are lessons. Some are seasonal. And some are keeping us from who we're becoming.

When you let go of what isn't aligned, you make space.
Space for clarity.
Space for new rhythms.
Space for rest.

It's not about cutting people off or quitting your job tomorrow. It's about recognizing who and what uplifts you—and what drains you. It's about understanding whether your current life reflects your current values.

Self-Reflection as a Tool

Self-reflection is where the shift begins. It allows us to notice our thoughts, behaviors, and patterns with curiosity—not judgment. In our personal and professional lives, reflection helps us grow with intention.

Take a moment and reflect on the past year.

- What are your glows (things that worked)?
- What are your grows (areas you'd like to improve)?
- What small change can you make this season?

Reflection is not about perfection. It's about clarity.

Mindfulness and Self-Care

Mindfulness teaches us to pause. To notice. To come back to the present moment.

Self-care teaches us to tend to what we find there.

As professionals—especially those in service roles—self-care isn't a reward. It's a requirement. You can't pour from an empty cup. And you shouldn't have to.

Mindfulness Practices

Meditation – Sit quietly for 5 minutes. Just breathe.
Mindful Breathing – Inhale, exhale, repeat. Center yourself.
Nature Walks – Get outside. Let the world slow you down.
Journaling – Write what's real. No filter. No edits.

Self-Care Practices

Physical – Move your body. Drink water. Get sleep.
Emotional – Call a friend. Laugh. Say what you feel.
Professional – Log off on time. Take your lunch break. Say "no" when needed.

These small actions matter. They reconnect you to yourself.

Personal Development Is Self-Care

Growth is a form of self-care. The Bible reminds us: *"People perish for lack of knowledge."* Sometimes, we're stuck because we haven't learned the tools to move forward. Other times, we're afraid to grow because it means we'll be accountable.

But growth doesn't mean fixing everything at once. It means learning better, doing better, and staying open.

You don't have to be perfect—you just have to be willing.

The Truth About Accountability

Let's tell the truth: sometimes, we stay ignorant on purpose. It's easier not to know than to face what needs to change. But healing isn't about comfort. It's about honesty.

And yes, sometimes it stings.

As I wrote this, I felt a few "ouches" too. But I've learned to see those as invitations. Invitations to reset. To be honest with myself. To grow again.

I've done this work—and I'm still doing it. That's what self-care really is: not spa days or silence, but choosing to show up for yourself. Every single day.

As Summer Winds Down…

As this season closes and a new one begins, I want you to take a breath and ask:

What did you lose when there was nothing to gain?

Maybe you lost time. Energy. Joy. Maybe you gave too much to something that didn't give back.

Now it's time to reclaim your power. Reclaim your peace. Reclaim your purpose.

You don't have to wait for January, or the next crisis, or the perfect plan. You can start now. Reset. Recenter. Reclaim your story.

You deserve to walk into this next season whole—not just for your students, coworkers, or clients—but for *you*.

Let go of what no longer serves you.
Embrace what brings you life.
And don't forget: you are allowed to change.

Connect With Lakeisha Lee

https://www.luv-lee.shop/shop-all
https://www.facebook.com/share/14LUVa9f7tr/?mibextid=wwXlfr
https://instagram.com/luvlee.naturals?igshid=YmMyMTA2M2Y=

$60

Luv-Lee NATURALS

ROOTED & RESTORED

A RETREAT FOR MIND, BODY & SOUL

SEPTEMBER 13, 2025
10 AM – 2 PM

MINDSPRING • 966 TUNNEL RD

register at: luv-lee.shop

BACK TO SCHOOL, BACK TO BALANCE: HELPING KIDS THRIVE EMOTIONALLY AND ACADEMICALLY

Shona Royce, M.Ed, LPCC, NCC, Helps Students Build Resilience, Routine, and Readiness

By Shona Royce

Back to School

Back to school can be a stressful and scary time for parents and students, especially for younger students or students starting new schools. My name is Shona Royce, and I am a Licensed Professional Clinical Counselor. I provide counseling to children in-office as well as in a school setting. I provide services for Attention Deficit & Hyperactivity Disorder, Oppositional Defiant Disorder, Adjustment Disorder, Generalized Anxiety Disorder, and more.

- **How do your services help students in school?**

I am very fortunate to work with some great school systems that allow me to see clients at school. This allows me to assist my clients/students with:
- Following directions better/on-task behaviors
- Independent living skills/social skills
- Emotional dysregulation
- Peer difficulties
- Good study skills/habits/organizational skills
- Transitions & more

- **Do you interfere with the student's learning?**

I typically do not see clients during their core classes. I typically obtain a copy of the client's schedule to ensure they are not missing core content.

- **Do you have any tips for parents whose children are returning to school?**

Have a set sleep schedule.
The more rested your child is, the better they will do in school. It may also reduce "crankiness" in the morning.

Have good organization.
Get clothes, backpacks, and shoes ready the night before. This cuts down on scrambling around in the morning.

Maintain good communication with your child's teacher.
Discuss expectations (teacher's, yours, and child's).

Start the school year out on a positive note.
The more positive your child sees you, the better attitude they will have.

Connect With Shona Royce
M.Ed, LPCC, NCC

https://www.roycecounseling.com

ACCELERATING SUCCESS: HOW SYEDA IS REDEFINING ONLINE SALES FOR COACHES

Magnetic Income Accelerator, led by Syeda, is dedicated to revolutionizing the sales and marketing landscape for online business owners, particularly coaches and consultants. With a background as a corporate sector manager and a passion for helping professionals excel in sales and marketing, Syeda embarked on her entrepreneurial journey one year ago. Since then, she has successfully assisted 35 clients in achieving their sales goals.

Magnetic Income Accelerator specializes in both inbound and outbound sales strategies, offering innovative methods to attract and engage potential clients. Syeda's magnetic strategies are designed to establish a strong online presence, drive organic lead generation, and optimize client acquisition processes. Through personalized coaching programs, she helps clients clarify their high-ticket offers, revamp their sales processes, and leverage AI-driven tools for effective lead generation on platforms like Facebook.

At Magnetic Income Accelerator, the focus is not just on generating leads but also on building strong, intuitive personal brands. Syeda's coaching program emphasizes defining brand identity, crafting compelling brand stories, and establishing influential online presences. By staying consistent and committed to the coaching program for 90 days or 30 days, as per the customized needs of clients, they can elevate their profiles and become influential figures in their respective industries.

Syeda takes pride in her ability to make a global impact through her services. One of her standout achievements was helping a client in Pakistan achieve remarkable success in online sales, demonstrating the reach and effectiveness of her strategies. Looking ahead, Syeda envisions Magnetic Income Accelerator continuing to grow and expand its reach, with a mission to assist online coaches worldwide in optimizing their sales processes and achieving their business goals.

Connect With Syeda Iqra

Facebook
https://www.facebook.com/share/18rdTMg6Lo/

Instagram:

https://instagram.com/syeda_iqra0000?igshid=OGQ5ZDc2ODk2ZA==

THE WOMAN IN THE MIRROR: FROM TRAUMA TO TRIUMPH

By Ciara Lewis CEO/Founder

Looking in the mirror has been a significant challenge for me over the past several years. This struggle stems from my experience in a domestic abuse relationship that stripped away a crucial part of my identity. Living in a constant state of fear, enduring daily negativity, and never knowing when the next eruption of violence would occur left me feeling paralyzed. The haunting sounds of someone entering my home, coupled with the terrifying memories of a person who was once my best friend becoming my worst nightmare, have profoundly impacted my life.

Stories like mine are often silenced by shame and fear. Yet, I have chosen to let my past be the foundation upon which I have built my resilience and strength. I refused to allow that chapter to define my existence. I took my life back, distancing myself from the toxicity, and I now thrive as if that darkness never existed. I share my journey not just for myself but to remind other women that recovery is possible and that they are never alone. Each of us navigates our struggles differently, but empowerment is attainable.

It took a stark realization to understand how much I had been robbed of—my friends, my family, and my sense of self. It became clear that I was being isolated, controlled, and manipulated. I reached a breaking point and declared, "Enough is enough."

I moved forward with the support of friends who stood by me, whose belief and understanding were vital during my darkest moments. His past relationships, surprisingly, also turned into a source of support. Relocating to my hometown and reestablishing familial connections provided me with a solid support system. Most importantly, my daughter became my anchor, guiding me through the storm.

To cope, I kept myself occupied, a strategy that proved essential during overwhelming times. For years, I was caught in shutdown mode, harboring anger toward men, waiting for a reason to lash out. This pent-up pain often led to sudden outbursts, a result of having been silenced for far too long. Initially, I vowed never to date again, to keep my distance from all men. However, as time went on, I found myself navigating the complexities of relationships anew, grappling with discomfort and frustration at the slightest comment directed at me. Each day was a lesson; just when I thought I had identified a trigger, a new challenge would emerge, reminding me of the lasting impact of my past.

At a pivotal moment in my life, I lost trust—not just in people, but particularly in men. I often questioned why no one came to my aid or tried to help me, only to realize that it was impossible for anyone to intervene when I had never spoken about the turmoil I faced behind closed doors. I kept my struggles to myself, believing it was my burden to bear alone. The harsh reality is that I had two best friends who would have undoubtedly stepped in, but shame and fear of my circumstances led me to cancel plans and withdraw from support.

Since then, I have made significant strides. I proudly raised my now 18-year-old daughter, graduated from college, and founded two businesses. I successfully completed the OMBW program with Goldman Sachs, and I was even featured in Forbes magazine alongside my cohort from the program. Has the journey been easy? Absolutely not. Every day has presented its challenges, many of which I still navigate today.

I have improved my ability to accept and acknowledge compliments, and I often take a moment to look in the mirror, treating myself with kindness and love. Rebuilding my capacity to trust others remains the most formidable challenge. I have entered a few relationships since those dark days—each proving to be a complex journey. While I still have much to work on, I am no longer imprisoned by fear or someone else's control. I now approach each day with reduced stress and can finally enjoy peaceful nights of sleep.

I am currently in a relationship, facing our own challenges rooted in my past. However, my partner is understanding; he respects my need for space and does not hold me accountable for past traumas. Having such support is crucial, even amidst the adjustments we both must make. There are still moments when I question certain actions, wondering if there are underlying motives, or I find myself anxious during disagreements, worrying about the potential for deceit or abandonment. The lingering fear of being left behind is real, and I recognize the need for constant reassurance—something my partner is more than willing to provide.

Reentering the dating scene requires patience from both parties. It involves relearning how to be kind to yourself and reminding yourself that you are safe—until proven otherwise. Not everyone is deceitful; in fact, many people are genuinely trustworthy. This mantra has been essential for me. I often defaulted to projecting guilt onto all men, living in a state of heightened defense for far too long. I still find myself slipping into that defensive mode without even realizing it. This journey is ongoing, but I stand strong and empowered, ready to continue moving forward.

About a month ago, my boyfriend and I visited Miami, where I discovered a boudoir photography studio seeking participants for a complimentary photoshoot. Intrigued, I applied, not expecting to be selected—especially while on vacation. However, three days before our departure, I received a call informing me that I had been chosen for the shoot. Seizing this unexpected opportunity, I recognized it as a prime moment to connect with like-minded individuals for my magazine and explore potential collaborations. During our conversation, it became clear this experience aligned perfectly with my magazine's mission. I felt compelled to embrace this chance, knowing that shying away would contradict the image I aim to promote to other women through my work. This leap into the unknown was undeniably bold for me; I typically avoid showcasing my body or skin, and it had been years since I had truly embraced my self-image.

The photographer offered me a choice between a striking black background with a red cover-up or a crisp white backdrop with a color of my preference. Opting for white—a choice outside my usual palette—seemed aligned with my vision for the magazine. The photographer echoed my sentiments, emphasizing that this decision would complement the theme of the magazine and serve as an inspiration for other women.

Participating in that photoshoot stands as one of the best decisions I've ever made. The environment was welcoming, comfortable, and invigorating. Upon entering, I was greeted with a red carpet and an elegant backdrop, alongside the option of refreshments—mimosas, coffee, or water. Although I declined the makeup and hair service, the atmosphere alone was invigorating. In the spacious studio, I selected a color that resonated with me, and the enthusiastic photographer pointed out that my nail color matched perfectly with the cover-up we decided on.

The team fostered a sense of safety and comfort that made me forget my surroundings, allowing me to feel empowered and in control for the first time in ages. Their encouragement to embrace my beauty and confidence transformed my perspective. I felt like a new woman, ready to conquer the world, realizing this is the confidence I should embody every day. Once the shoot concluded, the photographer escorted me to another room to reveal all of my photos, a moment that encapsulated the celebration of self-empowerment I had just experienced.

This is where I discovered my true strength. When she began to share the photos with me, I was overwhelmed with emotion. I had never realized that I could look like this—confident, with a figure that surpassed the negative opinions instilled in me. It was a profound moment of love and happiness that enveloped me. I was genuinely impressed with how the photos turned out. For the first time since my past experiences, I felt as if I was embracing every part of myself. I stood tall, exuding confidence and a sense of freedom, completely relaxed and authentic.

It was the first glimpse of the heavy chains that had bound me for so long finally being released. I saw the new woman I had become—one who radiated happiness and success—and it was an exhilarating feeling. This photoshoot became a powerful reflection and a memory I will forever cherish. It unveiled a new part of me, offering a fresh perspective on life and self. After selecting my favorite images, she presented me with a beautiful rose, a simple yet touching gesture that truly made my day. I can't recall the last time someone gifted me flowers for no particular reason.

**Photo Credit:
Nouvo Studios Miami**

REFLECTIONS OF STRENGTH: RECLAIMING MY POWER AFTER ABUSE

Photo Credit By: Nouvo Studios Miami

The essence of this experience lies in the reminder that we, as women, often lose sight of who we are amidst the myriad responsibilities we shoulder—whether as wives, partners, mothers, daughters, or business leaders. These roles can divert us from our true selves, leading us to neglect our happiness, self-care, and wellbeing. We frequently forget to pause and breathe, preoccupied with societal expectations. It's essential to remember that our purpose is not just to meet the world's demands but to honor ourselves first. We are our own best protectors and the only ones capable of cultivating our happiness. We must seize these moments of clarity, making the most of them, and remember to breathe deeply when necessary. We cannot be the best versions of ourselves and support others if we neglect our own needs. Some may think the pictures I am going to share from my photoshoot are inappropriate or uncalled for, but the point of my magazine is stop caring what others think and do you. Stop trying to conform to the world or how the world wants you to be and be yourself. I'm also sharing my experience, because I want women to see that the impossible is possible, it is safe to step outside your comfort zone.

I can try new things, and you can most definitely be comfortable in your own skin and image. The best part about all of this is that I did manage to partner with the owner, and in part of our partnership, they are willing to offer a free photoshoot for any women who feature or purchase our magazine and scan the QR code. They have several locations, and this is a once-in-a-lifetime opportunity. Thanks to Nouvo Studios Miami for helping me find a huge part of me that was missing.

Connect With Ciara Lewis CEO/Founder

www.linktr.ee/ninamotivates
www.youtube.com/ninamotivates

Saturday September 13, 2025

RNR D2 Summit Teams & Winslow Winery
PRESENT

For Tickets Text 724-880-7195 or on FB RNR Summit Athletes Fundraiser

Sparkle, Sip, & Win

Wine. Bites. Prizes. Good vibes.

🎟️ $40 Ticket Includes:
🍇 5 Wine Tastings
🧀 Each with a Perfectly Paired Snack
🎁 3 Chances to Win 1 of 5 Amazing Prizes!

Grab your friends and join us for an unforgettable evening of flavor, fun, and a little luck! Limited spots available—don't wait! 💫

Available for an additional purchase:
- Chinese Auction
- Loco Pop
- Breakopens
- More

LV Graceful PM

LV Victorine Wallet

$500 Cash

$500 Cash

Spa Package

Rostraver Central Fire Department
1100 Fells Church RD, Rostraver Township, PA
Doors open at 4:30

FIERCE & FEARLESS

COMING SOON

NEW PODCAST
Fierce & Fearless Women Entrepreneurs

Host
Ciara Lewis,
Entrepreneur & Author

Launching in June 2025!

Email:
Fierceandfearlessentrepreneur2025@gmail.com

NUOVO
ARTISTIC STUDIOS

Invest in Your Legacy today!

Resilience
COUNSELING SERVICES

ACCEPTING NEW KENTUCKY CLIENTS!

Building Your Mental Wellness!

At Resilience Counseling Services we prioritize YOUR mental health and Targeted Service Coordination needs. Our therapists are highly trained to meet the needs of each client. We accept most major insurance providers. Self-pay options are also available.

Kentucky Services

ADHD Services: ADHD diagnosis, assessments, and ADHD coaching.

Eye-Movement Desensitization and Reprocessing Therapy (EMDR): Reduces the power of traumatic memories and helps clients reprogram them with positive beliefs.

Therapy Services Tailored to the Following: Eating disorders, post/pre-bariatric counseling and coaching, depression, anxiety, PTSD, substance abuse, parenting therapy, family reunification therapy, and many more.

 606.485.4049

 Scheduling@WeAreResilience.net

Nationwide Services

ADHD, Bariatric, and Life Coaching: We provide various forms of coaching to people across the United States utilizing online sessions. These services help people build confidence, manage challenges, and reach their goals.

We offer morning and evening availability with both in-person and telehealth options.

TO LEARN MORE ABOUT OUR SERVICES, CONTACT US TODAY!

 www.ResilienceServices.net

 671 KY-80 Suite 2 Somerset, KY. 42503

Dear Daughter...
Your Story Was Never Meant to
Stay Silent

Are you ready to write your letter of faith, freedom, and legacy to the next generation? Email us to become a co-author! No writing experience needed.

Contact Us:
660.221.3370
mjdesigns@mail.com

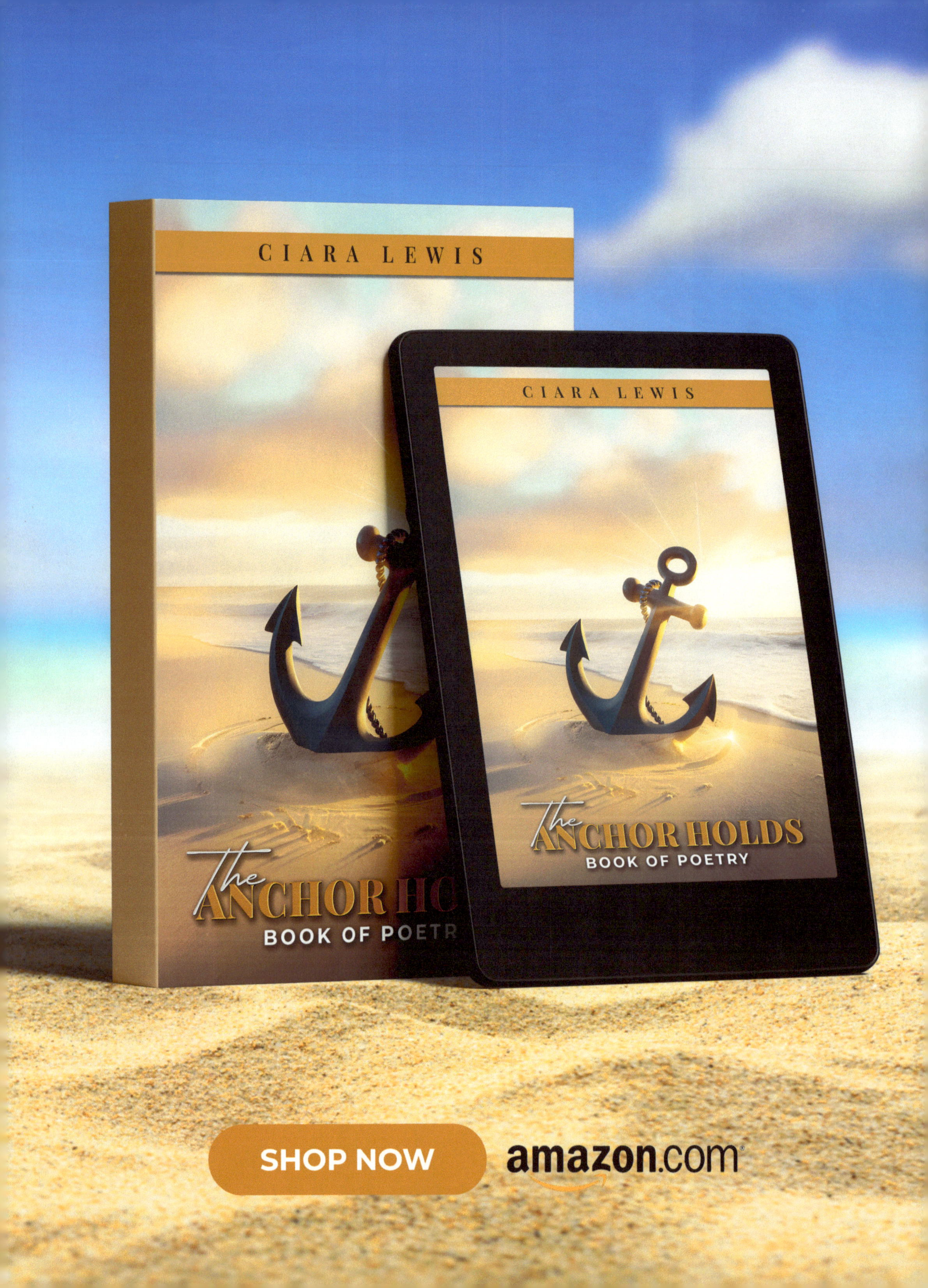
CIARA LEWIS
The ANCHOR HO
BOOK OF POETR
CIARA LEWIS
The ANCHOR HOLDS
BOOK OF POETRY
SHOP NOW
amazon.com

FIERCE & FEARLESS

BECOME A PUBLISHED AUTHOR!

Only $750!

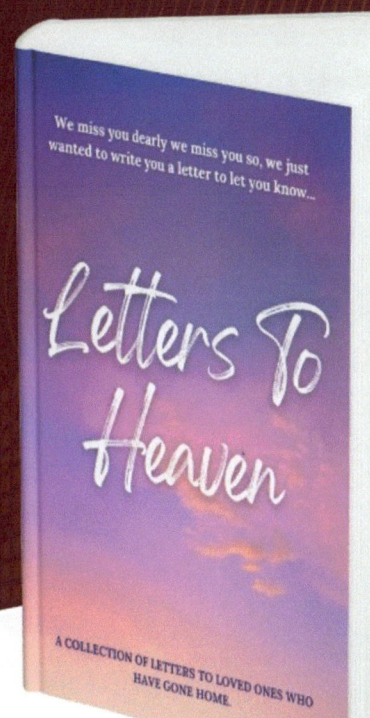

As an author, you will receive:

- Your story published in our upcoming anthology
- Exclusive gift: your choice of a custom mug or coaster
- Access to a virtual book release ceremony
- Invitation to a live book discussion with fellow co-authors

Ready to share your story with the world?

Join here:
fierceandfearlessentrepreneur.com

Spaces are limited – secure your spot today!

SCHOOL IS IN SESSION:

Essential Mental Health Strategies for a Successful Year Ahead

By Maria Crabtree

As a seasoned mental health practitioner with over 15 years of experience, I understand the challenges that accompany the return to school—not just for students, but also for parents. As a mother of four, I have firsthand insight into the anxiety and stress that can arise during this time. Students grapple with feelings of uncertainty about progressing to a new grade, adjusting to a different school, concerns about bullying, and the pressure of fitting in. For parents, the demands can be equally taxing, with the financial strain of purchasing back-to-school supplies and clothing, along with worries about their children's safety and well-being.

Reflecting on my own experiences of back-to-school jitters from elementary through college, I recall the fear that came with the unknown, coupled with a desire to thrive academically. I often questioned whether I'd be able to keep up with the material and find my place socially. An incident from elementary school lingers in my memory—being teased for wearing clothes from Wal-Mart. My mother's solution was to buy clothes from K-Mart, and while I appreciated her effort, it underscored the complexities of school dynamics. Growing up as one of three children, our family navigated the demands of back-to-school shopping by making it a fun event, despite the financial constraints.

While times have evolved, some resources remain familiar. My mother utilized layaway to manage our clothing needs, a method still available today alongside modern alternatives like AfterPay, Klarna, and Affirm, which provide similar financing options.

Throughout my educational journey, the most valuable lesson I've learned is the importance of authenticity. Embracing who you truly are is crucial and allows individuals to pursue their unique paths with purpose. However, the journey to self-acceptance is often riddled with challenges. Many feel compelled to alter their appearance or beliefs to conform to peer expectations, drifting away from their true selves.

During the pivotal middle school years, it's common for young people to seek their identities, often pulling away from parental influence and gravitating toward peer groups. As adults, we must champion and model authenticity for the younger generation. It's vital for us to embody our true selves and resist peer pressure, encouraging kids to do the same. Embrace your individuality and project self-love and confidence.

What are some effective strategies for fostering authenticity in ourselves and our children?

#1 Embrace Self-Belief
To cultivate self-belief, engage in daily affirmation and gratitude journaling. Acknowledge that we are human, experiencing a range of emotions, but do not allow negativity to impede your progress. The most significant dialogue you have daily is the one with yourself—ensure it's one that uplifts rather than diminishes. Your words act as powerful influences, akin to casting spells; what you declare into existence will manifest, whether positive or negative.

#2 Establish a Healthy Routine
A harmonious balance between physical and mental health is essential. Implement daily self-care strategies, including positive hygiene practices, regular physical exercise, a nutritious diet, and a consistent sleep schedule. These elements contribute to the best version of yourself. Remember, physical and mental well-being are interconnected, and you hold the responsibility for your own health.

#3 Foster Open Communication
Do not hesitate to express yourself if burdens weigh heavily on your mind. Open up to someone you trust—whether it's family, friends, or a mental health professional. Speaking up can provide relief and perspective.

#4 Recognize Triggers
Awareness is paramount for initiating meaningful change. If you are unaware of what requires alteration, transformation cannot occur. Tune in to your emotions in various situations; many people behave in ways that provoke reactions. Maintain control and preserve your personal power; never allow anyone to diminish it.

Connect With Maria Crabtree

www.Ascendinghealth and wellness.com

www.ingramcontent.com/pod-product-compliance
Lightning Source LLC
Chambersburg PA
CBHW041443010526
44119CB00042B/489